For Syl —
Happy days in
your "new" house —
Love from "Isi"

OUT
IN THE DARK
AND
DAYLIGHT

OUT
IN THE DARK
AND
DAYLIGHT

Aileen Fisher
BY AILEEN FISHER

Drawings by GAIL OWENS

HARPER & ROW, PUBLISHERS
NEW YORK

ACKNOWLEDGMENTS

First published in *Cricket, The Magazine for Children,* © Aileen Fisher: "Cricket Jackets," November 1973, © 1973; "Frosty Morning," January 1974, © 1974; "Cricket Song," July 1975, © 1975; "For a Ladybug," July 1975, © 1975; "Grass," April 1976, © 1976; "Out in the Winter Wind," December 1973, © 1973; "Mouse Dinner," May 1975, © 1975.

The following poems are reprinted by special permission granted by *Weekly Reader,* published by Xerox Education Publications, © Xerox Corp.: "After a Rain," © 1964; "April," © 1969; "April Fool," © 1962; "Before Christmas," © 1975; "Birds," © 1964; "Cocoon," © 1965; "Frosty Window," © 1963; "Listen, Everything," © 1965; "October Fun," © 1967; "Raindrops," © 1966; "Sparkly Snow," © 1965; "Winter Morning," © 1965.

The following poems are used by permission from *Weekly Reader,* published by Xerox Education Publications: "Christmas in the Country"; "Flake on Flake"; "Hinges"; "On Halloween"; "Spider Web"; "Spring Patterns"; "There Goes Winter."

First published in *The Instructor* magazine: "Snowbirds," February 1968.

Reprinted with permission of the publisher, Allen Raymond, Inc., Darien, Conn. 06820, from the April 1973 issue of *Early Years:* "Mouse House"; "At Night"; "Duet"; "To Be a Bird"; "My Puppy."

First published in *Expectations* (Braille Institute of America): "Autumn Concert," © 1970; "Sounds of Spring," © 1969; "Beetle Thoughts," © 1971; "Christmas Secrets," © 1970; "Frogs in Spring," © 1972; "Taking a Walk," © 1973; "April Bird," © 1974; "Clover Field," © 1975; "My Cat and I," © 1975; "Leaf Buds," © 1976; "Fall Wind," © 1976; "In the Sun and Shadow," © 1977; "Wind Music," © 1977; "Shoes," © 1979.

Library of Congress Cataloging in Publication Data
Fisher, Aileen Lucia, 1906–

Out in the dark and daylight.

Includes index.
SUMMARY: A collection of poems celebrating all the small things that make up every day.

1. Children's poetry, American. [1. American poetry]   I. Owens, Gail.   II. Title.
PS3556.I79308   811'.5'2   78-22492
ISBN 0-06-021902-5
ISBN 0-06-021903-3 lib. bdg.

T 12534

OUT
IN THE DARK
AND
DAYLIGHT

Out in the Dark and Daylight

Out in the dark and daylight,
under a cloud or tree,

Out in the park and play light,
out where the wind blows free,

Out in the March or May light
with shadows and stars to see,

Out in the dark and daylight . . .
that's where I like to be.

Speaking of Leaves

A *rhubarb* leaf
makes a very good hat,
or a parasol,
so remember that
if the sun shines down
on your sunburned nose . . .
and you happen to know
where rhubarb grows.

A *lily* leaf
on a pond is great
for a round green seat
or a flat green plate
that's anchored beyond
a mossy log . . .
that is, if you happen
to be a *frog.*

A leaf of *grass*
makes a very fine whistle
between your thumbs,
but, I warn you, this'll
not be the case
with a leaf of thistle.

Firefly

Firefly, firefly in the night,
when you flash your twinkly light,
do you know as you flit by
you're a *beetle,* not a fly?

Firefly, firefly in the dark,
do you know you have no spark,
not a spark of *fire* at all . . .
just a light that's cool and small?

Firefly, firefly, please come by
underneath the darkened sky,
blinking as you flit along . . .
even if your name is wrong.

Bumblebee

I sat as still
as a playing-dead possum
and watched a bee
on a clover blossom,

Watched him poking
his long thin tongue
into the blossoms
pink and young,

Heard him bumble
and sort of sneeze
as pollen stuck
to his two hind knees.

I held my breath
as the bee buzzed over,
and hoped *I* didn't
look sweet as clover.

Mouse Dinner

A mouse doesn't dine
on potatoes and beef . . .
he nibbles the seeds
from a pod or a sheaf.

He catches a beetle
and then gives a brief
little wipe of his mouth
on a napkin of leaf.

Under a Stone

In the middle of a meadow
we turned up a stone
and saw a little village
we never had known,
with little streets and tunnels
and ant-folk on the run,
all frightened and excited
by the sudden burst of sun.

We watched them rushing headlong,
and then put back the stone
to cover up the village
we never had known,
to roof away the tunnels
where ants were on the run . . .
before they got all sunburned
in the bright hot sun.

Walk at Night

Wouldn't it be fun
when the moon is bright
to take a walk
through the world of night
and peek in the windows
of hollyhocks and trees,
looking for the bedrooms
of birds and bugs and bees?

The Moon

My puppy looks at the big old moon
after the day turns dim
and probably thinks it's a bright balloon
with a face inside the rim.
He doesn't know about astronauts . . .
the moon hasn't changed for *him*.

To Be a Bird

I wish I could fly
through the sky with ease
and try all the seats
in the boughs of trees,

And look from a perch
on the highest steeple
at streets full of
upside-down cars and people.

Twice Born

For moths and butterflies, it's nice:
they get born once, they get born twice.

They get born first from tiny eggs
as caterpillars having legs.

They get born next from silk cocoons,
with *wings,* on summer afternoons.

If *I* should get a second try,
I'd like to grow some wings, and fly.

Grass

Do you ever think about grass
on the lawns you pass?
The green of it,
the sheen of it,
the after-raining clean of it
when it sparkles like glass?

Do you know what grass *is*,
those green spears showing
wherever you're going?

Every blade, to be brief,
is a *leaf*.

Summer Stars

Is a star
too far
for a rabbit to see?

Can his eye
see high
as the top of a tree?

It doesn't much matter,
for close to the ground
star-blinking fireflies
twinkle around . . .
in summer.

Birthday Present

No, not something
to read, or eat,
but something
with race-away, chase-away feet.

No, not something
to ride, or wear,
but something
with rumpledy, frumpledy hair.

No, not something
inside a bag,
but something
with something outside to wag . . .

That's what I want,
the best thing yet,
and that's what I hope,
hope, hope I'll get.

Wind Music

The west wind plays a merry tune
upon the pine all afternoon . . .
the music swells and ebbs.
I wonder if a little breeze,
too small to play upon the trees,
can play on spider webs?

My Puppy

I have a playful
prankish pup:

When I stoop down
he prances up

And snuffs my neck
and slicks my ear

As if I'd been
away a *year*.

I say, "Be good,
you prankish pup."

But he just smiles
and eats me up!

Cricket Jackets

The day a cricket's jacket
gets pinchy, he can crack it
and hang it on a bracket
as he goes hopping by.

He doesn't need a mother
to go and buy another,
he doesn't need a mother,
and I will tell you why:

Beneath the pinchy jacket
the cricket sheds with vigor
he has a new one growing
that's just a little bigger,
to last him till July.

And then, again, he'll crack it,
his pinchy cricket jacket,
and hang it on a bracket
as he goes hopping by.

How Big?

The sun, they say, is very big,
a star that shines by day,
much bigger than the whole big earth,
oh, *very* much, they say.

But when I'm hiding in a field
of clover-smelling hay,
a single little clover plant
can hide the sun away.

Daisy World

We saw a city of daisies . . .
a whole big daisy town,
thousands of white heads bobbing
and nodding up and down.

And off beyond the city
the daisy suburbs showed,
clusters of daisy neighbors
along a winding road.

And off beyond the suburbs
in sprinkles here and there
we saw the daisy farmers
enjoying the open air.

The Streets of Town

On a hot and lazy day
streets lie sleeping time away.

But when rain shuts out the sun,
streets jump up and start to run.

Mirrors

The sun must have a lot of fun
from dawn of day till day is done,

Seeing its bright and shiny face
in every puddle every place.

Picking Berries

All day long
we picked and picked.

The sun was strong,
the bushes pricked.

The berries grew
in brambly places
where twigs untied
my sneaker laces.

We picked and picked
and picked some more.
The sun blazed down,
my arms got sore,

And then all night
as time went ticking
I dreamed I *still*
kept picking, picking.

Night Out

Nobody knows
where Tim-cat goes.
Down the road? Or through the meadow?

Into the night
and out of sight
he hurries past the purple shadow.

At break of day
he's back to stay,
contented with our sunny dwelling.

But nobody knows
where Tim-cat goes
at night . . . and Tim-cat isn't telling.

Barefoot in the Clover

In the vacant lot
where the clover grows,
I can pick clovers
between my toes.

I can pick clovers
by twos and threes . . .
but not the ones
that belong to *bees*.

Penthouse

We climbed up a tree,
and know what we saw there?
A robin's old nest
full of twiglets and straw there.

We looked in the nest,
and know what we found there?
A penthouse of ants
way up from the ground there.

We said, "In the summer
how clever to be there,
high up in the cool
shady green of the tree there."

Listen!

Isn't a breeze
a thoughtful thing,
giving the trees
a chance to sing?

Sun Prints

The lawn is full of footprints,
golden tracks that show
where the sun went walking
a day or two ago.

My father calls them *dandelions*.
I think they're sun prints, though.

Taking a Walk

Don't you sort of wonder
when you take a walk
if chipmunks stop and listen
to people-kind of talk?

If birds and bugs and rabbits,
nearby or farther out,
cock their ears and wonder
what people talk about?

Hinges

A bird is full of hinges.
He needs them every day:

His wings hinge wide
on either side
and flap, and tilt, and sway.

His hinge-y neck
goes peck, peck, peck
upon the feeding tray,

And when he flies
he's always wise
to hinge his legs away.

Moonstruck

I'd like to see rabbits
under the moon,
dancing in winter,
dancing in June,
dancing around
while twilight lingers
and blinky-eyed stars
look down through their fingers.

I'd like to see rabbits
under the moon,
but I always,
always
have to go to bed too soon.

Buttons of Gold

Our lawn has a jacket
(but not for the cold),
a shiny green jacket
in place of the old,
with many more buttons
than jackets should hold . . .
just *look* at the buttons
of dandelion gold!

To Be a Clover

I wonder how it would feel
to be a clover
with a bee buzzing over
and landing in my hair
on three pair of tickly feet,
looking for something to eat?

I don't imagine it would hurt me.
It would be better
than having a grasshopper squirt me.

It would be better
than being a leaf
and coming to grief
if a caterpillar found me
and began nibbling, nibbling, nibbling
around me.

A Sandpile Town

Building a sandpile town with shops
and houses and churches with steeple tops,

And finding pebbles for paving streets,
and moss for gardens, and acorn seats,

Is always, always a lot more fun
than having a town that's finished and done.

At the Sandpile

How is it out at the sandpile
at night when the moon is shining?

Do our buckets and spoons and shovels
all have a silver lining?

Does moonlight brighten our castle
and bridge that the moat goes under?

Does a quick little mouse
slip out of her house
to see what we've built, I wonder?

Shoes

Shoes on our feet,
shoes on our feet—
two little houses
that walk down the street,

One story high,
not very wide,
two little houses
with feet shut inside!

Out in a storm,
cozy and warm,
two little houses
have work to perform,
                But
When it is fair,
June in the air,
who wants those stuffy
old houses to wear?

Raindrops

How brave a ladybug must be!
Each drop of rain is big as she.

Can you imagine what *you'd* do
if raindrops fell as big as you?

After a Rain

Leaves have such
a raincoat skin
raindrops cannot
sink down in,

And so the raindrops
sit about
and shimmer
when the sun comes out.

Waves of the Sea

Waves of the sea
make the sound of thunder
when they break against rocks
and somersault under.

Waves of the sea
make the sound of laughter
when they run down the beach
and birds run after.

Sky-Fish

Yesterday
we thought of fishing
when the lake was purpled-out.
But we didn't
take our fish poles
or our hooks . . . we went without.

Uncle Stephen
rowed the rowboat
where the moon made silver bands,
and our fingers
fished for moonfish,
but they slithered from our hands.

Then we tried
to catch the starfish
bobbing bright, with shiny scales,
but they dribbled
through our fingers
as they flicked their starfish tails.

Yesterday
we went out fishing
where the sky-fish glittered bright,
and I'm glad
we didn't catch them
so they'll still be there tonight.

In the Sun and Shadow

The hands of the sun
are warm on me
when I walk in the open meadow,

But the hands feel cool
when I pass a tree
and walk through the leafy shadow.

My Cat and I

When I flop down
to take a rest
my cat jumps up
upon my chest.

She kneads my sweater
with her paws . . .
and sometimes even
uses claws.

She rubs my chin
and purrs away,
as if I am
a game to play!

But I Wonder . . .

The crickets in the thickets,
and the katydids in trees,
and ants on plants, and butterflies,
and ladybugs and bees
don't smell with little noses
but with *feelers*, if you please.
They get along quite nicely,
but I wonder how they *sneeze*.

Garden Toad

Under a plant in my garden
I saw a wrinkled toad.
In fact, I saw him quite often . . .
he never thought he showed.

My father said, "Nothing is better
than having a toad till fall.
At night he catches the insects
on plants that are halfway tall."

But what did he do a year ago
when I hadn't a garden at all?

Mother's Helper

Dust has a way of hiding.
(I sometimes miss the clue.)
It hides in nooks and corners
and back of curtains, too . . .
and *that's* where Mother's sure to look
when I say, "Dusting's through."

Duet

I hold her close
and cuddle her
and rub my chin
against her fur
and then we both
begin to purr.

Cricket Song

Did ever you see
a cricket's ears
stick out upon his head?
You certainly didn't
since they grow
below his knees instead.

It's good he doesn't
put stockings on
and cover his knees up tight,
or how could he hear
the songs he sings
night after autumn night?

Pumpkin Head

We bought a pumpkin big and round
that lived the summer through
without an eye to look at things . . .
and *now* it looks through two.

It used to be all dark inside
when growing on the vine,
but *now* it has a toothy smile
and face that's full of shine.

Chipmunk

I saw a little chipmunk
scamper through the hay,
up a log, and down a log,
and over and away.

I tried my best to follow,
to look at him once more,
but he went home a secret way
and used his secret door.

October Fun

Who has a big and smiling mouth,
a tooth up north and two down south?

Beneath his mouth who has a chin
that's rather round and curvy-in?

Who has three corners to his eyes—
the strangest shape, the strangest size?

Who has a nose, three-cornered, too,
where orange light comes shining through?

On Halloween

We mask our faces
and wear strange hats
and moan like witches
and screech like cats
and jump like goblins
and thump like elves
and almost manage
to scare *ourselves.*

Autumn Leaves

I wonder in September
and in October, too,
what oaks and elms and maples
and quaking aspens *do*
to make their leaves
turn red and gold
instead of pink and blue?

Country Window

Look at it rain
on the windowpane!

Look at it splash
from the roof's mustache!

Look at it pour
on the field's brown floor!

We stand and watch . . .
and nobody cares
if it rains and rains
on the garden chairs,
the road, the clover,
the grass, the wheat . . .

It's raining puddles
for wading feet.

For a Ladybug

A leaf makes a roof
for a ladybug,
a house where she can huddle.

A twig or stalk
makes a road to walk,
and a drop of dew, a puddle,

And a tuft of fur
on a cocklebur
makes a bed where she can cuddle.

Toadstools

The elves put out their hats
one night
on poles so they could dry.

And next day
we discovered them
when we went walking by.

And Kevin called them
mushroom plants
or toadstools . . . but not I.

I said the elves
put out their hats,
their pleated hats to dry.

Beetle Thoughts

What do beetles think about
in places where they crawl?
Are their thoughts in April
like the thoughts they have in fall?

No one knows what beetles think,
but if they think at all
I think the thoughts that beetles think
must be very small.

Other Talk

There must be other kind of talk
that's not like ours at all—
sometimes blustery and loud
and sometimes wispy-small—
that tells the tulips when it's spring
and woodchucks when it's fall.

Autumn Garden

Now the gardens grow on trees,
now the year turns old:
crimson flutters in the breeze
next to green and gold.

The Quiet-Shining Sun

After the gusty, dusty wind
that blustered out of space
has whipped the grass
and flipped the boughs
and made the meadow race,

I see the quiet sun come out
and, with a patient face,
serenely pick the scenery up
and put it back in place.

Autumn Concert

In the evening
in the thickets

There are orchestras
of crickets,

And you never
need buy *tickets*

To hear concerts
by the crickets.

In the Snow or Sun

I wear outer clothes and inner,
sometimes thicker, sometimes thinner.

When the yellow days turn grayer
I wear layer after layer,
with a parka or a sweater,
or a slicker when it's wetter.

But a dog or cat or camel
or some other kind of mammal
like a woodchuck or a rabbit
has a less expensive habit,
wearing all its clothes *in one*
in the rain or snow or sun.

A Toad

I saw a toad with nobbly warts
of many kinds and many sorts.
She scrunched beside a boulder.

I heard for warts there is a cure
(Old Mr. Dinkle thinks "for sure")
and so I up and told her:

"A plain potato, toad, will do.
Just rub it on a time or two,
then bury it, to moulder,

"And all your warts will go away.
You ought to try it soon, today,
before your warts get older."

But I'm afraid she didn't hear
or didn't get directions clear . . .
she *still* had warts when I went near,
in spite of what I'd told her.

Rabbit in the Woodpile

The rabbit in the woodpile
is a rabbit safe and sound
in hidden rooms and tunnels
when a beagle comes around.

The rabbit in the woodpile
is a rabbit snug and warm
in hidden little cubbies
when it's threatening to storm.

The rabbit in the woodpile
is a rabbit weatherproof . . .
since *we* have just a little fire
to save his woodpile roof!

Stars

It's very hard,
oh, very hard
to cut a paper star,

And so I blink
each time I think
how many stars there are.

I look up high
and think, "Oh, my,
the stars are bright and fine,

But who had time
to make them all
and get them all to shine?"

Country Rain

The road is full of saucers,
saucers full of rain,
some of them fluted,
some of them plain,
saucers brown as coffee,
saucers full of sky,
saucers full of splashes
as our feet flump by.

Spiderweb

A spiderweb
snares bugs and flies
and insects of the smallest size
within its maze of swirls,

But once I saw
(when it had rained)
a web, all shiny, that contained
a rainbow trimmed with pearls.

Sky Rider

We saw a young little
daring spider
who lived with a
spinning wheel inside her,

Saw her sail
on a silken thread
over the meadow
just ahead,
over a field
and a patch of gravel,
riding a thread
too strong to ravel,

And I sighed
as I spied
her dip and glide:
"Oh, what a wonderful
way to ride!
Oh, what a wonderful
way to travel!"

Chirping

They say a cricket
chirps each note
by using neither
mouth nor throat.

He rubs his wings
and, as they scrape,
those chirpy cricket-
sounds escape.

I'd think his wings
would be a sight . . .
the way he uses them
all night.

Back to School

When summer smells like apples
and shadows feel cool
and falling leaves make dapples
of color on the pool
and wind is in the maples
and sweaters are the rule
and hazy days spell lazy ways,
it's hard to go to school.

But I go!

The First Day of School

Peter is often the first one up.
He's always the fastest eater.
But today he toys with his plate and cup . . .
it's the first day of school for Peter.

Peter is always the first one dressed.
He's faster than I, and neater.
But today he's certainly second-best . . .
it's the first day of school for Peter.

Peter looks down at his sweater cuff,
and his voice begins to teeter:
"Mom . . . is it hard? Will I know enough?"
It's the first day of school for Peter.

Next-Door Neighbor

She always has a treasure
hidden in a pot,
buried under special earth
from a special spot.

When the weather blusters
over field and hill,
she brings a pot of treasure
and sets it on the sill.

A tulip, amaryllis,
or don't-you-wonder-what?
She always has a treasure
hidden in a pot.

Early Moon

Some days the moon comes early,
at least an hour or two.
Her watch is wrong, or maybe
she hasn't much to do.

I've seen her palely waiting
upon a sky-blue shelf,
so white and sort of lonely
she isn't like herself.

But when the sun sinks westward,
and evening comes, and night,
she reaches out an eager hand
and switches on her light.

Thanksgiving Dinner

With company coming,
there's always BEFORE:

Hang the red peppers
and corn by the door,

Shine up the silver
and sweep up the floor,

Sample the dressing
and gravy once more . . .

Listen! They're coming.
Run, open the door!

Wind Circles

Without a pen,
without a hand,
without a pair of glasses,

The broken stalks
so bent and tanned
among the scattered grasses

Draw curves and circles
in the sand
with every wind that passes.

And *I*
can't draw them half as grand
in school, in drawing classes.

Fall Wind

Everything is on the run—
willows swishing in the sun,
branches full of dip and sway,
falling leaves that race away,
pine trees tossing on the hill—
nothing's quiet, nothing's still,
all the sky is full of song:
"Winter's coming. Won't be long."

Day and Night

When the sky begins changing
her dress for the night,
she does it so slowly
you can't see it quite.

But when she removes
from her velvety pocket
the silvery moon
that she wears for a locket,

And bright little sequins
of stars sparkle out,
you know Day is over
and Night is about.

Little White Birches

The little white birches
stand thin and bare
when frosty November
is in the air,
but *I* think birches
don't really care.

They're much too busy
with work to do,
packing their buds
all waxed and new
with leaves to open
when winter is through.

After a Freezing Rain

The brittle grass
is made of glass
that breaks and shatters
when we pass.
It clinks against
the icy rocks
and tinkles like
a music box.

Difference

On paper that's ruled
or plain and white,
with pencil in hand
we sit and write.

On meadows of snow
spread white and neat,
little *mice* write
with tails and feet.

Looking out the Window

I like it when it shines
on the oaks and pines.

I like it when it snows
and a white wind blows.

I like it when it tinkles
with sprinkles of rain
that crinkle the face
of the windowpane.

The Chickadee

The morning after winter
when bitter weather came,
the chickadee was cheery—
as cheery as his name,
but I should think he'd like a pair
of earmuffs, all the same.

Snow Party

Let's give a party
in winter, in the snow.
Let's ask special friends
and some we don't know.
Let's serve party food
and hope the guests will stay.
Let's ask *all the birds*
the first white day.

Winter Morning

A tablecloth all snowy white
is spread upon the lawn.
Without a sound it came last night,
and stayed when night was gone.

And now a flock of snowbirds comes
and settles in the trees,
hopeful for a feast of crumbs
and suet . . . if you please.

Going Calling

I didn't want to go.
I told my mother so.
I said I'd rather stay at home.

But how was I to know
they'd have those things to show
from Mexico and India and Rome?

And how was I to guess
they'd have a printing press,
and little silver half-a-dime,
and let me see the book
of photographs they took,
and let me play the sticks that chime?

Oh, can't we go again sometime!

Early Snow

When snow fell down
in a dance of white
roofs grew nearly
a foot last night
(I don't mean wider,
I mean in height).

Hills grew higher
beyond the town
with pillows of white
to hide the brown,
but *bushes* . . . the bushes
bent down
      down
         down.

Sparkly Snow

Last night the sky was reckless,
a reckless millionaire:
it threw down chips of diamonds
and strewed them everywhere.
And on this bright cold morning
when we go stomping out
footprints full of diamonds
follow us about.

Out of Season

All winter the cottage
just slumbers and waits,
and so do the kettles
and saucers and plates.

There's hardly a splinter
of sun on the floor
with shutters on windows
and locks on the door.

I hope that the Deer Mice
inside by themselves
find something for Christmas
on one of the shelves.

At Night

When night is dark
my cat is wise
to light the lanterns
in his eyes.

Noises

We play that we are soldiers:
Tramp! Tramp! Tramp!
We play that we are horses:
Stamp! Stamp! Stamp!
We play that we have boots on:
Scuff! Scuff! Scuff!
Till Mother tells us, "Quiet!
    Enough's enough."

We play that we know secrets:
Sh! Sh! Sh!
We play that we are whispers:
Sp! Sp! Sp!
We play that we are sleepy:
Yawn! Yawn! Yawn!
Till Mother says, "I wonder
    where everybody's gone?"

Mother Cat

Blackie is a mother
with a cheerful disposition:

Her kittens crawl all over her
and never ask permission.

They fight her and they bite her
with their tickly little teeth.

They maul her, and go crawling
up and down her underneath.

But Blackie doesn't care
if they frumple up her hair . . .

She only purrs and blinks
and takes her forty winks.

Snowy Benches

Do parks get lonely
in winter, perhaps,
when benches have only
snow on their laps?

Before Christmas

We sing, and plan,
and watch the date,
and write some cards . . .
and wait and wait.

We look for presents
at the store,
and make some, too . . .
and wait some more.

We wrap our gifts
and tie them straight,
and frost some cookies
on a plate,
and buy a tree
to decorate,
but most of all
we wait . . . and wait.

Frosty Window

The frosted window
shows tall white ferns,
and trees, and rivers
with twists and turns,
and strange white forests
with flowers of ice . . .
wish I could *walk*
in a place that nice.

Christmas Secrets

Secrets long and secrets wide,
brightly wrapped and tightly tied,

Secrets fat and secrets thin,
boxed and sealed and hidden in,

Some that rattle, some that squeak,
some that caution "Do Not Peek" . . .

Hurry, Christmas, get here first,
get here fast . . . before we *burst*.

Flake on Flake

Softly, softly, day and night
flakes of snow fall featherlight.

Flakes of snow fall light as fluff,
yet when they pile deep enough

They send spruces to their knees
and break the backs of tall old trees.

Good Night

Father puts the paper down
to say good night,
and his mustache prickles
when he hugs me tight.

Mother sets her knitting bag
beside her chair
and asks me if I've washed myself
and brushed my hair.

Grandma says, "Keep covered.
Sweet dreams to you."
And I feel quite sleepy
when "good nights" are through.

Frosty Morning

The water in the birdbath
is icy-shiny now,
so birds can skate instead of drink,
that is, if they know how.

Christmas in the Country

Run, little wild ones,
over the snow,
peek through the trees
where yourselves won't show,
look at the lights
on our Christmas tree,
brighter than any
stars you'll see!

Out in the Winter Wind

Puff! Puff!
Wind is a gun
shooting the fluff
from the pines for fun,
sending the snow-smoke
toward the sun . . .
turn up your collar
and run, run, run!

Snow on the Wind

The winter wind carries
white feathers, white fairies,
white frost-flowers that whirl through the air,
white stardust, white petals,
white cotton that settles
on everything . . . everywhere.

The winter wind scatters
white fluff in white tatters,
white dancers who twirl on their toes,
white snow-elves who caper,
white stars of white paper,
white snowflakes . . . that melt on my nose.

Snowbirds

Do you wonder, do you wonder
what snowbirds find to eat
when seeds are buried under
little hoppy, scratchy feet,
and branches all are snowy
in the yards along the street?

Shall I tell you, shall I tell you
what snowbirds think a treat?
Crunchy crumbs and suet
and corn that's cracked, and wheat . . .
and someone at the window
to be watching while they eat.

Winter Stars

Winter is the time for stars:
for hours and hours they shine
on sparkly fields and icy ponds
and snowy roofs, like mine.

They shine before it's dinnertime,
and on till breakfast's due . . .
I think they must get very tired
before the winter's through.

Pussy Willows

Willow buds come early
while snowflakes still are swirly
and maps of snow are still around
in the shadows on the ground
and skies are cold and pearly.

The buds are in a hurry,
but dress so warm and furry
in their glossy snuggle-ins
zippered tight around their chins,
they never have to worry
about arriving early
while snowflakes still are swirly.

There Goes Winter

There goes Winter
sloshing off
with puddles in his tracks.

Here comes Spring
on roller skates
with jumping ropes and jacks.

Muddy March

Watch your step across the field,
hop from stone to stone.
The only crop these acres yield
is mud, and mud alone.

Now that frost is in retreat,
not a spot is dry.
March wears wet and muddy feet . . .
and (squish, squish!) so do I.

Looking

We poke around and pry about
and try to find a tiny sprout
where greening has begun,

We search along the privet hedge
and up and down the garden's edge
to where the grapevines run,

And then we give a merry shout
and cry, "Come, look—a crocus out!
As yellow as the sun."

Spring Pictures

Spring paints pictures in the town
and on the waking hills,
using tints of green and brown
and gold of daffodils,
now a sweep of sparkly light,
now a touch of gray . . .
Spring paints pictures left and right
and gives them all away!

Spring

When you see a daffodil
and know it's spring,
all the songs inside of you
begin to sing.

Cinderella Grass

Overnight the new green grass
turned to Cinderella glass.

Frozen rain decked twigs and weeds
with strings of Cinderella beads.

Glassy slippers, trim and neat,
covered all the clover's feet . . .
just as if there'd been a ball
with a magic wand and all.

I Brought My Mother Buttercups

I brought my mother buttercups
one day when she was weary.

She said I brought the sun inside,
all shiny-bright and cheery.

And then I saw her wink at me,
and then I heard her mutter,
"I'm glad there's *sun* in buttercups
instead of plain old butter."

Listen, Everything

Ting-a-ling-a-ling,
listen, everything:
winter's gone, it's spring!
Time to grow and sing.

Meadow, cock an ear.
Hurry, flowers, appear!
Rabbits, get your baskets out . . .
Easter's almost here.

The Noisy Wrens

Our wrens are back,
and how they scold
before the wren-house door!
They dart inside
and loudly hold
debates, then scold some more.

Then Jenny Wren
and John, her spouse,
make sticks and twiglets fly.
"A winter mouse
has used our house.
The nerve of him!" they cry.

Up There in the Dark

Stars come out
at eight or nine
(in fall at six or seven),

Stars, of course,
come out to shine
to light the way to heaven,

For, otherwise,
it wouldn't show
up there in the dark, you know.

Looking Around

Bees
    own the clover,
birds
    own the sky,
rabbits,
    the meadow
    with low grass and high.

Frogs
    own the marshes,
ants
    own the ground . . .
    I hope they don't mind
    my looking around.

In the Wind

We heard a jay
and we heard a robin,
and found new green
in a brown old knobbin,
and saw new sleeves
of the willow sway,
and smelled the river
a mile away.

We felt a breeze
that was mild and yellow,
and watched a flicker—
a noisy fellow,
and found new grass
where the old grass lay . . .
and smelled a *picnic*
for Saturday.

Barefoot

Let's pick clovers
between our toes
out in the yard
where the clover grows.

Let's pick dandelions
made of gold
out in the shade
where the grass is cold,

Or pick up pebbles
if we should choose
out in the yard
when we get to use
our birthday feet
instead of our shoes.

Let's.

Early Bee

Early bee, April bee,
where are you going?
I can't see, early bee,
very much growing.
Not a head, white or red,
shows on the clover,
not a bloom with perfume
all the field over.

Early bee, April bee,
where are you gliding?
Do you think food and drink
linger in hiding?
Oh, I see, early bee!
My, aren't you clever.
Nectar and pollen
from *catkins.* I never!

Robin Song

I know what the robin
sings in the morning,
sings in the ear
of the rising sun:

> "Hurry up, hurry up,
> nighttime is over.
> Hurry up, hurry up,
> day has begun!"

I know what the robin
sings in the evening,
sings in the ear
of the setting sun:

> "Cheerio, cheerio,
> thank you for coming.
> Thank you for all the good
> shining you've done."

Birds

Mouths of birds are very strange,
but eyes of birds are stranger:
one eye looks for things to eat,
and one eye looks for danger.

All That Sky

Wouldn't you think
the birds that fly
would lose their way
in *all that sky?*

Petals

Flowers need petals
with cracks between,
a number of petals—
from three to 'teen.

And I know why!
To keep the cup
of a rained-on flower
from filling up,

Filling up
and toppling over,
bumping its head
on the grass and clover.

Easter Daisy

I went for a walk
when the day was nice,
and thought, "Spring's coming."
I thought it twice.

Then I saw a daisy
that was small and round,
close to the earth
on the snow-patched ground,

And the daisy said
to my secret ear:
"Coming, you say?
My dear, it's *here*."

Mouse House

Do you ever wish
you could look in the house
of a shy little, spry little
white-footed mouse
with six little mouselings
still quite new
who didn't know mice
were afraid of you?

In Payment

A caterpillar nibbles,
nibbles at a plant
until the leaves look ragged
and even rather scant.

And then the caterpillar
weaves a silk cocoon,
and turns into a butterfly
one sunny day in June,

And *then* he carries pollen
to blossoms red and pink,
which sort of pays for nibbles
that he nibbled, don't you think?

Once a Year at Easter

Once a year, at Easter,
we like to climb the hill,
buttoned up and zippered
against the springtime chill.

We have to get up early
and cross the darkened lawn
and climb the nearest hilltop
to see the Easter dawn.

We know the old sun rises
each morning faithfully,
but once a year, at Easter,
we like to go and *see*.

Ears

Do rabbits and donkeys
whose ears stand tall
hear more than horses
with ears more small?

And what about bassets,
the ears *they* grow?

And what about robins
whose ears don't show?

April

The snowman's buttons are undone,
he's lost his wooden mouth,
for there is April in the sun
and wind is from the south.

The snowman lacks a coal-black eye,
an arm has fallen down,
for there is April in the sky
that loops above the town.

The snowman dwindles in the sun
and slowly falls apart . . .
but no one cares, for everyone
has April in his heart.

Overlooking

I went to find a rabbit
in the meadow near the brook,
but I watched a lazy lizard
and forgot to rabbit-look.

I watched a tomcat hunting
for a mouse that slipped from view,
so I almost missed the rabbit
who sat looking, looking, too.

Spring Joke

Rabbit, that's a joke on you,
hunching down the way you do
underneath a bush or tree . . .
can you blame the chickadee?

She wants fur to line her nest.
Rabbit fur, of course, is best,
so she takes an eager peck
at your hunchy furry neck!

Plenty of Time

As day sinks slowly past the trees
and paints the sky with red,
there's plenty of time for birds and bees
to find themselves a bed,

Plenty of time for ladybugs
and ants and butterflies
to hide in leaves or grassy rugs
with sunset in their eyes,

Plenty of time for serenades
from robins perched about
before the last of the sunset fades
and the first of the stars peeks out.

If I Had a Pony

If I had a pony
with a coat of velvet black,
I'd lead him out of winter
and leap upon his back.

I'd ride him down a meadow
and through a stretch of pine—
a cloud would make a shadow,
the sun would make a shine.

The air would smell of rainbows
and robin-birds would sing,
and I would tell my pony,
"It's spring today. It's SPRING."

April Fool

April started out to cry,
teardrops struck the pool,
frowns and furrows filled the sky,
all the air turned cool,
but a blinky moment after,
April, full of sudden laughter,
giggled, "April Fool!"

Cocoon

I found a little sleeping bag,
a brown one, very small,
found it dangling from a twig
like something left from fall.

I knew that it was waterproof
and silky-snug and dry,
and that the one who slept inside
would someday wake and fly,

And wondered if I'd ever see
him flitter-flutter by.

Clover Field

The smell of clover
is in the air,
spreading the news
that everywhere—
in every beckoning
clover top—
nectar is urging
a bee to stop
to sip a drink
and dust its clothes
with pollen to spread
wherever it goes.

Baby Birds

We found a nest of sparrows
with only *mouths* inside,
mouths of red and yellow
that opened up so wide
their parents couldn't miss them
even if they tried.

Wings

Bees have four wings,
birds have two,
I haven't *any*
and that's too few.

Frogs in Spring

Maybe they're glad
for the warmth of spring—
that's why frogs
in the frog pond sing.

Maybe they're glad
to jump and leap
after their long cold
winter sleep.

Maybe they're glad
to see their friends—
that's why they sing
when winter ends.

Maybe they're glad
to *eat* once more.
That's what *I*
would be gladdest for.

Answers

What weighs the littlest
you can think?
What hardly weighs at all?

"An aspen leaf," says Jennifer,
"that flickers down in fall."

"A milkweed seed," says Christopher.

"A thistledown," says Clive.

"A butterfly," says Mary Ann,
"and it's alive . . . *alive*."

April Bird

What is he singing, the April bird,
high in the maple tree?

Singing a song to please his mate,
wherever his mate may be?

Or singing because the sky is blue
and the breeze is fancy-free?

He's singing to say, "I want it known
this tree belongs to *me*."

That's what he's singing, the April bird,
high in the maple tree.

Sounds of Spring

Frogs that croak
and birds that sing
and peeper calls
are sounds of spring.
Day and night
our eager ears
are full of cheeps
and peeps and cheers.

But sap that flows
and buds that break
and seeds that split
and plants that wake
and other sounds
with quiet habits
only reach the ears
of *rabbits*.

Leaf Buds

All winter in the tree buds
the little leaves lie packed,
with tiny coats of April green,
all folded and exact.

And when the time is ready
(I wonder how they know?),
they quietly unfold themselves
and break the buds, and grow.

Lady of Night

Quietly down the sky,
quietly skirting the meadow,
the Lady of Night slips by,
trailing her purple shadow,
moving without a sound
of footsteps or garments sweeping,
wrapping her cloak around
birds in the treetops, sleeping.

Index of Titles